As the Curtain Falls

How to Die Consciously and Prepare for a Good Afterlife

SUE HAGAN

Copyright © 2022 by Sue Hagan, Suehagan.com
ISBN 978-0-9989182-0-4 print
ISBN 978-0-9989182-1-1 ebook
Library of Congress Control Number: 2022909055

Design and layout by Val Sherer,
          Personalized Publishing Services
Cover design by Susan Searway Art & Design, San Rafael CA
Clipart courtesy FCIT http://etc.usf.edu/clipart

Printed in the United States of America

Contents

Soul in Transition *(poem)*   ix

Introduction   1

Chapter 1: Universal Truths and Consequences   21

Chapter 2: Coping with the Transition to Come   37

Chapter 3: Staying Connected With Yourself
       and Others   53

Chapter 4: Moving Closer to Death   67

Chapter 5: Breaking Through   77

Chapter 6: Beyond Life on Earth   91

Chapter 7: On Remembrance Rituals
       and Celebrations of Life   103

Chapter 8: Preparing for a Good Death
       by Living Well   115

Bibliography   125

About the Author   129

Soul in Translation

Nature, nurture,
and the soul—
not two, but three—
a person, whole.

Sometimes it's smooth,
sometimes frustration,
no simple task,
true soul's translation.

Genetic characteristics,
the circumstances of our lives,
aide us or defeat us,
though the soul transcends, survives.

It's our soul we start and end with,
birth to death, not all, you see.
This life, a loan we're given,
then the soul's again set free.

Genesse Bourdeau Gentry

from *Stars in the Deepest Night–After the Death of a Child*
published by Writers Club Press

used by permission of the author

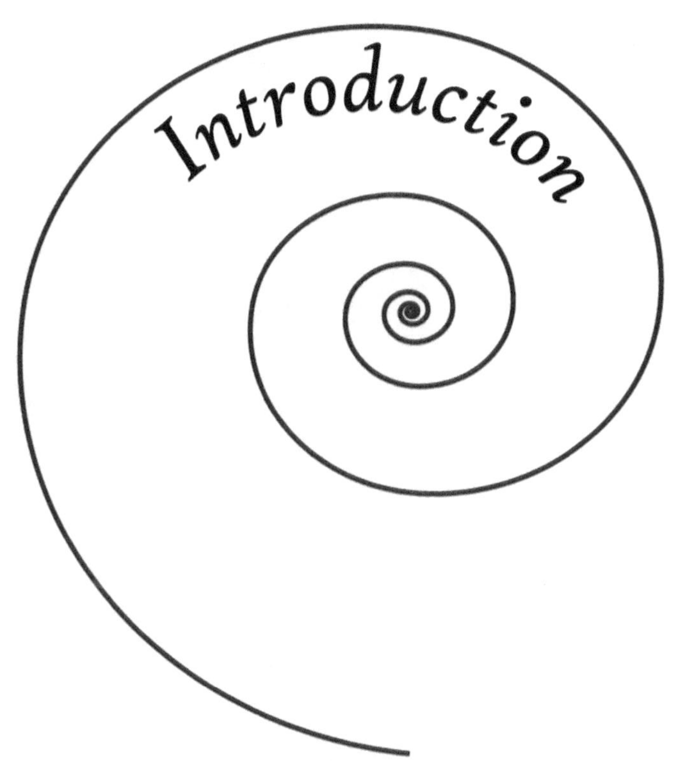

Introduction

Why Another Book About Dying?

Like many people, I have often found myself ruminating about death with fear and anxiety. Yet I didn't want respond to losses in my life from a place of fear, nor did I want to make my own end-of-life decisions burdened in this way. So I began to explore the subject of dying consciously. In this book, I provide my personal insights about the dying process and my understanding of what actually happens at the moment of death. By sharing my beliefs with you, it is my hope that you will start the process of examining your own beliefs and come to your own conclusions about life and death.

How am I qualified to speak on this subject? I am not a physician or a religious leader; my interest is not professional, it is deeply personal and experiential. Like many of my fellow baby boomers, I didn't encounter death at close hand until I reached middle age, when several family members and dear friends passed away. Through these experiences, and especially through caring for my parents and later my only sibling in their respective final days, my views on death and dying evolved. I have learned that the time leading up to a loved one's death can be incredibly significant and meaningful even while filled with bittersweet longing and sorrow. It is my intention to honor this last act of life through writing this book as a primer for the dying: straightforward, accessible, and intended for anyone interested in learning how to die well.

Asking the Big Questions

"What does it mean to not exist?" queried my sister from her hospital bed. Her physician had just unexpectedly told her that she had terminal pancreatic cancer and only a few days to live. As my only sibling, my sister and I shared an unusual closeness, and the thought of losing her was overwhelming. At first I didn't know how to answer her question. First of all, I knew that she had a fairly casual relationship with religious dogma and probably wouldn't find solace if I started quoting from the Bible. The one thing I felt I could tell her with certainty was that she would be joining many beloved family members

who had already departed. I knew this because I had a near-death experience of my own years earlier. Over the next few days, my sister left the hospital, went into hospice care, and eventually died peacefully at home. I stayed at her side, trying to maintain the strong emotional bond between us through constant prayer and hoping to provide reassurance about what was coming next for her. I tried to answer her question—*what does it mean to not exist*—through physical and emotional care, through sharing the story of my near-death experience with her and through constant reassurance that I would accompany her on her journey to the other side for as long I could. After her death, I thought to myself that someday I would take the time to collect my thoughts about death and write them down so that other people might find comfort in the words that gave solace to my sister.

My Own Near-Death Experience

In the mid-1980s I was married, pregnant, and enjoying a career in finance in New York City. Based on instructions in my prenatal support class, I anticipated that labor would be a difficult process involving a little pain. Assuredly, it would be nothing more demanding than a challenging aerobics class, and breathing exercises would make any pain go away, right? Was I wrong!

After hours of fruitless, induced labor I found myself laying on a narrow table in an operating room while doctors performed an emergency

Caesarean section. Because of my pregnancy complications and sensitivity to anesthesia, I was awake during surgery but not feeling much pain—initially. Complications arose after the baby was delivered. I found myself in excruciating pain. By this time there were several anesthesiologists in the room—they had appeared out of nowhere! I couldn't imagine what I had done to warrant so much attention. I remember telling the primary anesthesiologist that I couldn't hang on much longer. All of a sudden, I felt myself rising out of my physical body and I felt myself shooting down what appeared to be a brightly lit cylindrical raceway. From there, I looked down at the operating room and saw hospital personnel hovering over me. I totally "got" the emotions they were feeling toward me, as if I could read their senses before I understood what they were doing on a physical level. I felt touched to know they were rooting for me to pull through. It seemed like a very sweet gesture. At that point, I turned away from the scene in the operating room to see a figure appear from the shadows. Other beings were coming up behind the figure. I recognized my grandmother as one of those beings. She had passed away only a few weeks before. She and the others seemed startled to see me, and they conveyed to me that I must return, that it was not yet my time to join them. Suddenly, I felt a big swish of energy and I was pushed back into my physical body. Rejoining with my physical body required what felt like superhuman effort. Once in my body again, I felt constrained by its denseness and I missed the freedom of being without it.

Over the next few days, I recovered my health and I was sent home with my newborn son. Shortly after that, I went back to work. The days and nights blurred together as I managed the overwhelming demands of a challenging job and a colicky infant. I sometimes thought about what had happened to me in the hospital, when I left my body during surgery, but I didn't share it with anyone. I didn't know how to describe it, and it felt highly personal in a way I couldn't convey. Plus, it made me feel unbalanced and irrational to think that my mind or my consciousness had jumped out of my body, and I was certain that other people would call me crazy if I mentioned it. When I did later share the experience with a few people, including my husband, they thought I had made it up or suggested it was a hallucination brought on by all the drugs I took during labor.

Still, the near-death experience left a lasting impression. Once you have tapped into that non-material world, it changes you profoundly. Months later, I picked up a magazine containing an article about near-death experiences (NDEs) and the research being done on them at the University of Virginia Department of Psychiatry. Based on the examples in the article, it appeared that my personal experience seemed to be a truncated version of what other people typically encountered during a near-death experience. Intrigued, I wrote to the university and offered to be a participant in their long-term study.

Based on that long-term study, I found it reassuring to learn that my experience was not unique but in fact fell in line with the typical NDE. It is not uncommon, I learned, for the experience to feel very real, even though the person having it feels transported to a world with a different concept of time than ours. Many others also described making a life or death choice from a place of relative calm. When I left my body and traveled down a tunnel and encountered spirits of the deceased, I felt a combination of peacefulness, relief, and love, and I came to a point where I either had to stay or return to my physical body.

My NDE opened my mind to the existence of the spiritual world as something that I could tangibly feel. I had been raised in the tradition of Protestantism, but I can't say I knew with one hundred percent certainty that I was more than just a physical body until I experienced the NDE. Ironically, this increased awareness came with a feeling that I must stay silent about it. I believed that others would ridicule me if I spoke of it. So, while I was willing to anonymously participate in a scientific study about NDEs being conducted in a university setting, I never acknowledged publicly what had happened. Until now.

Spiritual Stew

Over the course of my adult years, I have peeked under the covers of various spiritual beliefs. Moving away from my mainstream Protestant upbringing, I dabbled in metaphysical workshops and spiritual traditions outside my culture. I studied meditation and developed my intuitive gifts at the Academy of Intuition Medicine in the San Francisco Bay Area. Then I became a student in the Diamond Approach, where I learned to use inquiry to tap into the divine essence within myself. Eventually, I studied thanatology and end-of-life issues in an academic setting, receiving a Certificate of Thanatology from Marian University in Wisconsin. Recently, I have returned to my mainstream Protestant church—well, I never really left it—and took on leadership roles in spiritual care in the community.

Each of us has a spiritual life and practice, conscious or not, that is a kind of stew—a mixture of experience, training, and aspiration drawn from any number of sources. Many of us have inherited from the culture a secular notion that death is something to be feared and avoided, and that when our time comes, we simply discard our physical body and cease to exist. Based on my NDE experience and my personal spiritual beliefs, I found myself wanting to share my thoughts on dying with others as an antidote to this way of thinking.

How to Use this Book

This book can be a guide through the transition of death, both for the dying themselves and also for loved ones. There are, of course, many causes of death and many ways to die. Readers with illnesses that are likely to result in death will find this book speaks to them. This book will be useful, too, for loved ones of the chronically ill as well as for people whose loved one has died unexpectedly due to an accident or a medical condition, such as a heart attack or stroke. (Chapters 6 and 7 may be especially helpful in these cases.) You may want to read one chapter at a time or you may want to breeze through it. You may want to read it out loud with loved ones. You may want to keep it as a reference book to consult when needed. I encourage you to read this book from your heart and decide what rings true for you and what doesn't. Take what is of service to you as a spiritual being and in alignment with your truth and leave the rest.

Whether dealing with an anticipated death or an unexpected one, the common thread is the transition from one form of being to another: the physical to the spiritual. In this book, I present the most universal touchstones of the dying process and address many commonly shared experiences of the dying—and the living.

I hope that you can start to view the dying experience in a holistic way, and within the context of your entire lifetime—however long that is. In meditating on death, you may come to the realization that we all would do well to get as much out of life as we can, because it won't last forever! As I point out at the end of this book, the real secret to dying well is to live fully.

When the time comes, I hope that what you learn in these pages will bring you and your loved ones comfort and ease in the journey across the bridge into the Infinite.

Chapter I

Universal Truths and Consequences

~

Perhaps you are facing a serious or terminal medical condition. Or perhaps an experience with a loved one's passing has inspired you to wonder what happened to him or her and what lies ahead for you when your time comes.

What happens when we die? Or, as my sister questioned, what does it mean to no longer exist?

Do we have an immaterial soul that survives death?

Is there life everlasting?

Even as we accept the inevitability of death, why do we fear it? How can we overcome that fear?

Some aspects of dying remain a mystery, of course, for all of humankind. None of us knows how it will happen, when it will happen, or in what state of mind we will be during the experience. Still, there are reassuring universal truths that can help as we travel, or consider how we will travel, the mysterious path to the other side.

It is Reasonable to Fear Death

It may be helpful to agree that being afraid of death is a rational, even healthy, response to an event that will eventually affect everyone living on the planet. What is it about death that we fear? The first characteristic of death that we fear is the process of dying. For better or worse, we don't know how long we have to live or when we will die. This unpredictability may increase our anxiety level, along with uncertainty about the circumstances of our death, the level of pain we might experience, and the availability of emotional support and medical resources, among other things. Depending on our circumstances, it may be reasonable to fear that we will be a burden on others, especially if a long-term, chronic disease is involved.

Secondly, the idea of being dead may provoke fear, especially if you believe that you are going to be punished for bad behavior and wind up in that special place called hell. Or, even if you don't think you are headed to hell, you may still be fearful that you are going to be deprived of all of the pleasurable aspects of living.

I believe, however, that for many people the thought of dying throws us into a state of confusion that resembles fear because we really haven't given much thought to what happens when we die. While we rely on the certainty of science in our daily lives, science hasn't proven the existence of a soul beyond our bodies, so that system of thought might not provide the insight we crave. On the other hand, it takes a leap of faith to believe that we are more than just a physical body acting like a mechanical system. To believe we are more than the sum of our physical parts, we must move beyond materialistic, science-based thinking and toward a more spirit-based philosophical or religious approach.

Since the time of Plato and Aristotle, philosophers have asked questions about the true nature of human existence, with the meaning of death always a major focus. If even the most brilliant philosophers and religious/spiritual leaders across the centuries can't agree about the nature of death, what's an ordinary person to do? The answer is to listen with your heart. As you read the rest of this chapter, see if any of the following ideas resonate with you.

Spirit Survives Beyond Death

Consciousness, or spirit, is indestructible and survives the death of the physical body. Without a body, consciousness is transformed in some ways, but you still remain "you" when the dying process is over.

During the dying process, a lot of things happen inside your body. Your physical systems are shutting down. When all of your physical systems have shut down, you can be declared officially dead. But other things are happening in other systems, systems outside of your physical body. Because our daily lives engage the physical body (especially the brain) to such a great extent, people don't tend to think much about what else exists besides the physical body. It takes effort, and perhaps a dose of imagination, to consider the dimensions of ourselves that are not physical.

Consider this: you are a unique human being. Some people might say that you are unique because of your engaging personality, your great smile, or some special talent you have. Scientists might say you are unique because of your DNA structure and how you were "put together" in a working physical body. However, what fundamentally sets you apart from all other human beings is your unique spirit.

Your spirit resides in your physical body, giving it conscious awareness. Some religions and spiritual schools call this the soul or personal consciousness. Your unique consciousness enters the physical body at the first moment of existence, typically creating a deep bond between offspring and parents.

Throughout your lifetime, your individual consciousness constantly interacts with others', starting within the family unit and spreading out from that point. You may not be accustomed to thinking about your relationships in this way, but you may intuitively recognize that as you grow up, you gain valuable experience from interacting with other people in widening circles.

From a spiritual standpoint, every interaction may be a valuable learning experience for the soul—even negative events that cause pain and suffering. Why then, you may wonder, have people who are very spiritually evolved, like those considered prophets in major religions, sometimes retreated from society on a temporary or permanent basis? They were not shying away from pain and suffering; they were limiting their outward interactions in order to focus on their internal connection with the Infinite. That time away, however, is not the only way to achieve spiritual growth. The vast majority of us must go to school, or work, or take care of business. We don't have to leave civilization and live in a cave in the desert.

If we stay committed to a practice of daily meditation or prayer, we can reach our spiritual potential. It takes hard work, but the rewards make it worthwhile. If we don't take the time to connect with ourselves and the Infinite, then we cannot claim our birthright as a soul to live as fully as possible through interactions with others. Giving and receiving love is the key to spiritual growth and evolution, and each person should strive to stay connected first to themselves, providing a foundation from which they can expand their connection with others.

Consciousness Returns to the Infinite After Death

~

A *soul's return* to the Infinite represents a homecoming—a return of individual consciousness into the boundless force field of universal consciousness. In many respects, it is easier to "live" on the other side, in spirit, because you are no longer navigating the complexities of modern life, not to mention that death puts you beyond reach of physical pain and assorted types of suffering that accompany life in a physical body. Instead, on the other side, wondrous loving forces surround you with absolute comfort on an emotional and spiritual level. Your spirit, this everlasting aspect of your life, survives physical death. In my view, this is how we know and feel the blessing and compassion of the Infinite. It is in the very nature of our individual spirit—essential and indestructible.

The living spend a lot of time daydreaming, reworking past events or relationships in their minds. Once you have passed over, there is no need for this. You do not dream about the future as you used to. The living spend a good part of their lives planning for their futures, motivating themselves to get through school, or master work situations. After you die, your focus shifts. You no longer care about the next job, the next report card, whom you should or should not marry, or when the best time to have children or retire might be. After you die, you will be led to review your life on earth as it truly was—your actions and your impact on others—and you will be held accountable in a loving and non-judgmental way.

Chapter 2

Coping with the Transition to Come

When you come to grips with the fact that you have passed the point of returning to good health and you understand that you are not going to live much longer, the world may feel like it has cracked open and you are being swallowed up in the void. To further complicate things, you may feel insecure or vulnerable, experiencing intense feelings at a deeper level than you have ever experienced. There may appear to be no end to the depth of your grief and sadness as you contemplate your death. It can feel like an anchor, sinking into a sea with no bottom. Added to this mix might be changes in medication (such as opioids, anti-depressants, or chemotherapy drugs) that affect your general state of awareness.

What's Happening Here?

From one moment to the next, your emotions can fluctuate, and how you respond to them may not feel under your control. You may vacillate between feeling calm and accepting and feeling wildly terrified. You may be defiant, rejecting the idea that this is really happening. You may be uneasy, or feel you are jumping out of your skin. Medication may further enhance or exaggerate these chaotic feelings.

These are some emotional experiences common among those who are in the process of dying:

- You may be ready to leave your body; you have been expecting this transition for a long time. Or you may feel the opposite, like this is some kind of bad dream and you don't belong here.

- You may realize you can't overcome the illness that is ending your life. You may begin to feel acceptance.

- You may feel that you don't deserve to be in this situation—you are dying. You may ask yourself why this is happening to you and not to someone else. (It actually is happening to someone else: several hundred thousand people die every day.)

- Your emotional responses may pile up on each other, leaving you confused as to what you are actually feeling.

- You may be filled with regret, thinking about how careless you may have been with your life, how you may have taken your existence (and possibly your relationships) for granted.

- You may think about how much you love this life and don't want to leave it. You may wistfully wish to turn the clock backward to a time when you were healthy.

- You may be afraid your loved ones won't be able to cope with your departure. You worry about them.

A Note About Anger

You may find that anger is the predominant feeling that arises during this period. You might want to let it rip on anyone in your line of vision, releasing everything from a minor annoyance to the most major, red-hot, blow-the-top-off kind of rage there can be. I invite you to use your anger as a signal that it's time to dig deeper inside yourself and find what lies underneath. Usually it's sadness.

The depth of your anger and rage may shock you, not to mention those around you. When these feelings overtake you, before you launch into a diatribe, you might ask your loved ones for permission to vent in front of them. This will minimize emotional damage, giving them a chance to decide if they feel balanced enough to handle your feelings and enough time to mentally don some armor before they listen. Be prepared if they *don't* want to listen to you in that moment. If you don't have a human to connect with about anger and it can't wait, try talking to a plant, or a mirror, or a stuffed animal. Or write in a journal as a substitute.

Intention to Participate
in Decisions

You may feel that things are completely out of your control—that you have no say in the fact of your death. Paradoxically, the way to counter this feeling is to actively involve yourself in decisions about your own care. You have the right to your own individual beliefs, and your loved ones and your health care team must respect those beliefs. You may want to develop and act upon a "bucket list" of activities you would like to do before you die. You might set up formal or informal ways of preparing your family members for your death. This may also be an opportunity to create a ritual to help heal

broken relationships, or a time for making plans

for the type of funeral arrangements you want

upon your passing.

The Spiritual Meaning of Your Life

As you consider your impending death, it is vital that you review the spiritual meaning of your life. What exactly does this mean? Consider the principle that you are a conscious spirit occupying a physical body. This may be a new concept for you, or it may already resonate with your belief system. Having religious faith can guide you on this question, but even if you don't have faith in a particular tradition, or if you are not especially introspective, pondering the spiritual meaning of your life can help with your transition. Challenge yourself to develop a spiritual narrative about where you stand right now in your relationship with your soul self, drawing on your life experiences to date.

Here are some ideas to assist in this endeavor:

• If you are accustomed to using prayer, you can pray for the blessing of time to allow you to learn as many lessons as you can in this lifetime before you pass over. You are, after all, still functioning on the physical plane, though you may be aware there are other, non-material things happening as well.

• If prayer or meditation doesn't work for you, experiment with other mindfulness techniques. These might include focusing on breath and slowing down your breathing. Listen to inspirational music, or play a musical instrument, to activate your higher consciousness. Do something physical like swimming or walking or sitting under a tree to help you empty your mind.

• Look for things to be grateful about in this world. Gaze at the stars or take in a beautiful sunrise or sunset. Recall awe-inspiring visits to a favorite park or beach or mountain.

• You can express gratitude for the time you have already spent on earth learning about and experiencing life. Be grateful for the difficult times as well as the good times, for all experiences have taught you lessons that you needed to learn.

• Trust in the knowledge that you receive
from your higher self, and trust yourself as
an instrument of the Infinite.

You walk in the footsteps of millions of others
ahead of you. Know that the entire time you are
transitioning, you are being held at the highest
level of love and compassion in the universe. You
are not alone.

Chapter 3

Staying Connected With Yourself and Others

~

When you are actively dying, the time leading up to death may be full of surprises regarding your relationships with others. It is important to nurture yourself and be honest with those around you. This can be a time of great opportunity and growth in your relationships.

Build a Network of Supporters

As you become more physically dependent on family and friends, you may find that your feelings for them change. People you have known for a long time will likely treat you differently than when you were well and functioning independently. People you barely know may be in your life as a team of health care workers coalesces around you. While you will most likely want to lead or manage these changes, you may feel ill-equipped to do so. You may feel like an outsider to your own life, that the floor has slipped out from under you, leaving you only partially present. You may feel like a changed person compared to when you were healthy. And you are.

What can help? Try to find at least one person with whom you can be completely honest. Ideally, this would be a family member or friend, but others can serve the purpose — health care workers, faith leaders, or other people you trust and respect. Share your grief with this person about all you are leaving behind. This allows you to keep your heart open as your body proceeds toward decline.

If you cannot find one person who is capable of holding you in this sacred way and giving you space to feel your intense feelings, perhaps you can find several people who can partially support you on a particular issue. This will enable you to weave together a band of supporters to serve the overall purpose.

Try to remain open to what people are offering, even if it misses the mark. They are doing their best to support you. Above all, be honest with others about what you really need.

Stay focused on kindness and compassion; they have many benefits. You may be moved to write letters to your loved ones expressing your appreciation for the gifts they have brought to you during this lifetime. When you stay focused on kindness, it encourages others to focus on their love connection with you, though their sorrow will want expression, too. Feelings of grief and loss in anticipation of your departure will likely be intertwined with love. Expressions of grief from your closest friends and family may take you by surprise, or they may happen with an intensity that rattles you. Do not minimize anyone's sadness and sense of loss, but rather share in their feelings. It's fine to cry together.

Be honest with your loved ones, too, about how much you can bear to hear or deal with. This is a tricky piece to navigate, but you have to take care of yourself above all others. You must not sabotage your well-being. You can always kindly remind your loved ones that there are resources besides you for expressing or sharing their sorrow. Perhaps you can identify someone to run interference for you if things get too intense. It is not your job to rescue others from their feelings.

Make Peace with Your Past

If emotions from recent or long-ago losses or traumas surface at the end of life, causing additional stress on all systems and taking focus away from the transition, deal with them in a positive way. You may want to contact people with whom you have unresolved issues and make amends, or bless them for the lessons you learned from those relationships. If you cannot connect with them in person or by a written or electronic form of communication, you can always convey your message in prayer or meditation. It's also not too late to seek professional help, such as psychotherapy or other support programs.

Similarly, if you are privy to family secrets or stories that you have been holding onto but would like to reveal before your passing, ask yourself if the other people involved would benefit from knowing the truth. Most of the time, revealing the secret releases the pent-up emotion around a hidden issue, and in the long run is a positive step. Sometimes you will find that others have sensed that there was something "off" about a family situation, but couldn't put a finger on it. However, it may be prudent to check with a trusted advisor or professional counselor if you have doubts about revealing a family secret.

Bear in mind that making peace with your past is always worthwhile; you will discover when you are on the other side that the Infinite supports any move toward wholeness and emotional balance, and honors your hard work in this regard.

Keep a Strong Connection with Yourself

Resolve that you will not abandon yourself during this time of transition. It may feel appropriate to distance yourself from your own sensations and emotions, because you may not recognize your once strong and capable body in its now diminished state. You may want to "escape" mentally as your crazy-busy life fades away and your world shrinks into a dull routine, focused around duties related to your health. Be vigilant about treating yourself with love, kindness, and compassion—just as you would extend that consideration to others.

Reflect on how you would treat a friend going through the dying experience just as you are doing. You would probably treat your friend with great patience, kindness and acceptance. You would overlook their negative behavior, irritation, impatience and emotional volatility. You are being called upon to do the same for yourself. Maintaining a healthy emotional balance through self-love is difficult under the best of circumstances, but it may seem almost impossible when you are dying. You may discover, however, as you are pulled away from ordinary life toward the other side, that there is a bottomless pool of self-affinity and compassion available to you.

While anxiety is a common feeling that surfaces during this time, be aware that you might also experience full-blown depression. Feel free to communicate with your health care provider about your mental state. There is no shame in taking medication or seeking counseling during this important time of your life.

Staying connected with yourself also involves recognizing that you have managed great challenges and transitions before. On a basic level, dying is simply another challenge—one you can handle. Recall how you managed significant changes in your life in the past, and identify the qualities that helped you move through them productively. This is part of dying consciously. Everything you have learned in your lifetime—how you handled disappointments as well as successes—plays a part in how you respond to the challenge of dying. That said, dying involves unanswerable questions and a level of mystery that is not subject to resolution or easy answers. Trust yourself to do your best, and turn the rest over to the Infinite.

Chapter 4

Moving Closer
to Death

~

When you become certain you cannot recover, and your hope for living much longer is gone, you realize there will be an actual date and time when you die. Because you love yourself and have committed to not abandoning yourself no matter what happens, you accept these circumstances.

Acceptance is Positive

Unfortunately, when it comes to the subject of death, the English language relies on metaphors from the battlefield, like "giving up," "surrendering," "fighting until the end," or "losing the battle." Yielding to the dying process does not, however, mean giving up or giving in. It means graciously and kindly accepting that soon you will be in a new state of being. You may feel disappointed or angry when people imply that you are not trying hard enough to stay alive, that you are "giving up." Even well-meaning people may say the wrong things to you. It's okay to tell them that, if you want to.

You know what is happening: you are following a natural progression from one kind of existence to another.

Dignity and Grace Continue

~

As self-respecting human beings, we are drawn to living and to dying with dignity and grace. As you become more dependent on others, however, feelings of vulnerability and shame may arise that detract from your goal of dying with dignity and grace. Moreover, during the dying process you may find yourself acutely sensitive to the feelings of loved ones who gather around you. At the very moment you feel deep sadness about your failing physical capabilities, you may also experience what you feel are negative emotions on the part of your caregivers (especially family members) who might find themselves performing caregiving tasks that overwhelm them physically and/or emotionally. This doesn't sound like a set-up for optimal dignity and grace!

Yet if you consider what is happening on a spiritual level, you will see that your capacity to receive love and care is increasing, and so is your loved ones' capacity to give unconditional love and support to you. Holding this spiritual explanation in mind during trying times, even if you lose control over bodily functions, will support you in maintaining dignity and grace to the end.

Pain and Isolation Disappear

Do not fear pain. There is no physical pain on the other side; there is only relief from any physical pain you experienced when you were alive.

You may feel like you are alone and heading toward total oblivion. You are not. The Infinite understands and accepts you completely. As you transition, you will find that your terror and anxiety are transformed into tranquility.

You are going to the place of ultimate safety, a place where you will see the bountifulness of the universe. Do not be afraid. Instead, invite the unknown as you step into the unfamiliar and mysterious realm beyond this life.

Remember that you are loved, both by the living and by those on the other side. Loved ones who preceded you in death may appear to you. Many care facilities report residents or patients seeing deceased loved ones in visions. These events are, unfortunately, often recorded as patient hallucinations. In truth, they are real sightings. You might see your own loved ones on the other side in this way, and these visions can reinforce the knowledge that you are not alone. At this stage, it can be a profound gift to sense the presence of departed loved ones around you. They are here to welcome you to the other side.

No one dies alone. *Ever.*

Chapter 5

Breaking Through

~

The Infinite cherishes each human's will to live, but when the time comes for that life to end, a door to another kind of existence opens. Everyone experiences this stage in his or her unique way. As the familiar life in a cherished body drops away, a new kind of being—previously unknown and hidden from view—comes into view.

Blurring Lines

As death approaches, you may experience a premonition of it. You may feel something unexpected is happening to you. Or you may notice a more general sensation of unrest or agitation. Feel whatever comes up, and, if you like, share your feelings with trusted friends and family members. You are entering a momentous and sacred passage.

I think of this time as the crossover stage, or breaking-through. The line between life and death blurs as your body and soul go through their own individual processes, beginning to separate. You might feel that you are seesawing between 2 places: one moment taking tentative steps forward into your future existence, then retreating back into the familiar surroundings of life in a body on earth. During this stage, you may feel an unexpected and overwhelming sense of love for life on earth and immense sadness at leaving it behind.

If you have been ill, you may feel like your body has taken the reins from your consciousness and is inexorably driving you to a termination point. Further, the road may not run smoothly or evenly, and loved ones or caregivers on watch nearby may see you struggling mightily at times and other times see you appear peaceful and accepting.

The act of dying occurs on more than one level at a time. While each physical body may follow a certain order as systems shut down (for example, the liver and kidneys may cease functioning before the heart), the process of releasing the consciousness follows no obvious pattern. Your consciousness has its own set of experiences and expectations, all which inform your spirit's relationship to the dying process. This can also affect the process of crossing over—for example, if you have attended at the deaths of others, or if you carry trauma about the moment of death of someone dear to you, these experiences can shape your own expectations. Everyone has his or her unique spirit that goes through its own process of separating from its beloved physical body before returning to the Infinite.

Sudden Death

If you are subjected to overwhelming pain and suffering because of an accident or an act of violence, the usual pre-transition experience described in Chapter 4 may not apply. To spare you unbearable pain and trauma, the benevolent Infinite may allow your consciousness to come over to the other side even before your physical body fully dies. Regardless of how little advance warning you have, understand that on a spiritual level, you will still die with dignity and grace.

Right Timing

The exact timing of your death is the "right" time for you. However, timing and death has gotten more complicated in recent years. Medical advances enable people who cannot breathe on their own to continue breathing with the help of life support machines, and expanded legal rights allow the dying and their families to determine with a medical provider when to turn off life support or when to administer a lethal dose of prescribed medications in states where that is legal.

Religious beliefs can come into play as well, because some religions oppose medically assisted dying or assisted suicide on the grounds that it interferes with the natural course of events and the divine will of God. There are also economically driven concerns that may affect decisions about the timing of death. In a market economy like ours in the United States, one that values productivity levels and monetary outcomes over intangible outcomes such as spiritual growth, common practice may be to defer to secular economic or material priorities while ignoring spiritual arguments for keeping a person alive.

Additionally, we all must strike a delicate balance between the desire to spare oneself or a loved one an infirm existence that appears pointless from the outside (and that might also be filled with pain and suffering), and, on the other hand, the need to acknowledge that there may be spiritual lessons still to be learned at the very end of life—for both the dying and his or her loved ones.

What can you do? As you plan for your own death, you need to make as many advance preparations as possible so that your wishes are carried out. Your health care team can advise you on the likely course of your illness and possible medical issues that may arise as you approach death. You need a written advanced care directive that specifies your desired medical interventions at any step in the process, should you become unable to communicate. In creating this document, you will have a chance to articulate your preferences. You may want a natural death with little medical intervention, or you may feel strongly that you want the option to end your life through the deliberate taking of prescribed medications.

Above all, you need to affirm with yourself that whenever your time comes, it will be the right time for you.

Can you bring that thought into your heart? It may feel scary or overwhelming to make these plans, but it can also bring enormous peace of mind. By blessing the end-of-life decision making—whether it is ultimately you or a family member in charge of that decision—you free yourself to live the remainder of your life with the highest level of integrity and intention.

When the Door Closes

When your consciousness leaves your body at the time of death, it shifts to a different viewpoint in another dimension. Everything you are aware of slows down, and you simultaneously experience everything more clearly and vibrantly on a sensory level. As the life force moves away from you, you begin to feel another force, one of love and longing, that propels you forward. You may also, at this time, feel a surge of gratitude for the body you inhabited and are leaving behind.

At the moment you pass over, the door immediately closes behind you. Your consciousness rises from your physical body and will not return to occupy your body. You will not be able to communicate with loved ones in the way you did when you were alive.

Family members and friends who attend to you may sense your spirit's detachment from your physical body. This may be profound and painful for them. They may experience your moment of death—the spirit's detachment from the body—as a single, powerful explosion of energy. Some may feel that you are gone in a sudden and indescribable way. Some may recognize that something significant has occurred, even if you had been unresponsive and/or unconscious on a physical level. What are they sensing? They are observing the transformation of the spirit energy, which has been contained in the physical form, rushing back to the Infinite as pure energy.

Chapter 6

Beyond Life On Earth

~

Welcome to your new existence! You never thought it was possible to exist without a body, but there you are, doing just that.

On the Other Side

As you break through to the other side, you find another world awaits you. You may experience a deep sense of coming home.

Or, panic may strike. Where have you landed? What happened to your "real" life on the material plane? Where is your body? You may try to return to your former existence, only to be met by an impenetrable wall.

It can take time for this new condition of being to sink in; your old existence on earth is over. While the severing of your consciousness from your physical body may feel like a cataclysmic event, the saving grace is that you are surrounded by the purest form of love, beyond anything you experienced on earth. If you allow yourself to surrender to what is happening, you will find that there are no hard landings when you enter the Infinite.

All of this may make you wonder about heaven and hell, as so many of us have been raised to respect or fear these places. Heaven and hell are tangled religious and spiritual concepts people have believed in and disputed for centuries. They are moral concepts that help guide the living, not actual afterlife homelands for the dead. After death, from all available evidence, your spirit will likely dwell in a realm that is pleasant and positive. This is the divine Infinite.

Now that you have passed over, you may see departed family members and friends, along with other beings you don't recognize. These souls are taking identifiable form to help you make the transition. People who have had near-death experiences—like myself—describe these types of sightings, and report that they contribute to a sense of peacefulness and acceptance about moving into the afterlife.

In the Presence of the Benevolent Infinite

Time exists in a different dimension in this world. Like a baby learning to stand upright, you must learn to adjust to this new state without a physical body. And, just like a baby taking his or her first steps, your spirit will lead you toward your new destination in its own way. Some spirits can't wait to start running pell-mell into the new existence, while others retreat and metaphorically sit down and pout!

The Infinite creates whatever scenario is needed to draw you in and bring you comfort, and each soul receives exactly what it needs.

Just as some people have more difficulty than others have in dealing with change, some spirits require more time to adjust to being without their physical bodies than others do.

As a newly returned spirit, you have unique characteristics that distinguish you from others who are recently deceased. For instance, if you were resistant to accepting help from others or you were accustomed to being the caregiver of others in your lifetime, your spirit may find all of this new attention and love uncomfortable and off-putting. Or you might be so anxious and tense about leaving your earthly existence behind that the experience leaves you distressed instead of euphoric. Eventually, you will find that accepting love and compassion will open your (spiritual) heart even more and bring you joy and peace.

Existence in the Infinite

In the crossover to the other side, you move away from an earthbound state of dreaming, planning and doing and settle into a state of reflection and understanding. It is as if the horizon flattens, and as it does, your perspective changes. The labors in your physical body are a thing of the past; they are behind you. As a conscious spirit, you are doing spiritual work now.

In many respects, existence in the Infinite is less complicated and easier than it was when you were alive. Any feelings of loneliness and abandonment experienced at the end of life have dissolved, replaced by a state of benevolence and compassion not available on earth.

Chapter 7

Remembrance Rituals and Celebrations of Life

~

Conventional wisdom says that memorial services are for the living. However, it is equally important for your spiritual development after your death that your loved ones come together as a group to celebrate your life and send you best wishes for your journey into the other side. These may be called many things: celebrations of life, remembrance rituals, memorial services, or funerals, among others.

Important for Everyone

The group dynamic of these celebrations helps to amplify and project positive energy, which in turn encourages your spirit in its transition to the new realm. Additionally, this group energy serves as a reminder that your time in your physical body is over and it is fitting for you to stay with the Infinite. The ritual is also a reminder that you will not be forgotten by your loved ones on earth. You see how much your presence in their lives mattered; even as a spirit you remain open to receive their love and appreciation.

Rituals also serve as a reminder that you can always communicate with the living through spirit-to-spirit connection. Accepting your new state does not mean completely moving away from your loved ones. As a departed spirit, you are "recalled" every time a heartfelt prayer or thought is sent into the Infinite from grieving loved ones. Your loved ones may sense your presence during their time of mourning, and for some time afterwards.

You may feel the tug of a loved one who holds onto you after your departure. You may ask for help from the Divine to lovingly allow him or her to remain on the living side and release you. Their life purpose cannot be fulfilled if they are preoccupied with keeping tabs on you in the crossover state. This may constitute a major task for your loved ones: being able to recognize that the dreams and hopes they had with you (and for you) are gone, and accepting that those dreams will never bear fruit, will constitute a major task for your loved ones as you lovingly watch over them from the other side.

Some people express a preference that no memorial service or group prayers and blessings take place after their death. A variety of factors may be at play for someone to reach this decision, ranging from concern over expense or travel time to a desire to avoid being made a fuss over. Alternatively, a person may have no affiliation with a religious organization or spiritual path, or they may want to avoid conflict among surviving family members who would come together at such an event. Regardless, remembrance rituals do serve an important function from a spiritual standpoint, no matter how humbly presented or informal they may be, for both the living and the deceased.

Make Your Wishes Known

~

While you are still capable of decision-making, make sure that your financial and legal affairs are in order. This may include your will and your advanced health care directive, which should incorporate a Durable Power of Attorney for Health Care. In certain situations, a POLST form (Physicians Order for Life-Sustaining Treatment) may be recommended to you. You may also want to complete a Five Wishes form, which addresses your legal and medical needs and also includes information about your personal, emotional, and spiritual desires. (See the Bibliography for information about where to find these forms.)

If you want your loved ones to be fully prepared, check out the information required to complete a death certificate in your state, such as full names and birth states of both of your parents, and give that information to family members so they will have it at hand when the time comes.

If it feels right, consider expressing your preferences about your future memorial service—the venue, music, readings, list of invitees, or even suggesting words that you would like those present to say about you.

You might consider writing down the major points of your life story to leave to your family as a memento. It may also help them in preparing to speak about you at your memorial service and/ or writing your obituary for publication.

Let your family know exactly where you want your remains to be laid to rest—in a cemetery, mausoleum, or returned to family. If you have a preference for a certain type of burial or cremation service or dispersal of ashes, make sure to express it to your loved ones. From the standpoint of the Infinite, there is a neutral stance toward how the physical body is treated after death. In other words, you don't get penalized if you want your ashes scattered at sea or you want to donate your body to a medical school for research instead of being buried in the family cemetery plot.

Still, standardized burial/cremation practices are an integral part of religions that have evolved over many centuries, and are a viable and important option for many. Alternative arrangements, such as family-directed home funerals (which share much in common with funeral practices in existence up until the twentieth century) might also be available in your area.

Lastly, don't forget to consider the tangible items in your life. If you own material possessions that may cause conflict or controversy among family members or friends after your death (and don't forget items that hold sentimental value as well as those that have monetary value), consider making your wishes known. Specify distribution to particular individuals in your will, or assign new ownership before you pass.

Let a trusted person know what you are thinking. Your loved ones will be grateful that you have made decisions and not left them guessing as to your desires.

Chapter 8

How to Prepare for a Good Death By Living Well!

~

You can't bargain your way out of death and you can't avoid having to face it: if not soon, then eventually. We all die. You can buy life insurance, you can take care of financial, legal, and personal matters you leave behind, but you can't buy a guarantee for a good death. How, then, should you get prepare? Live well.

Recognize Ways in Which You Have Already Lived Well

If you worry that you have not lived as well as you hoped, I would suggest you take a closer look. We are not accustomed to patting ourselves on the back for a life well lived. But that is exactly what I am asking you to do! When you consider the effort you have put into being a good son or daughter, doing well in school or at work, being a good friend, cooperating with your siblings, loving your romantic partners, caring for an animal, and appreciating natural joys such as being in the outdoors, wouldn't you agree that you have done an awesome job? Maybe you weren't perfect, but you applied yourself and did your best. Think of the times you were kind to a stranger or reached out to help a friend or family member. Every one of those experiences count, and they definitely outnumber the times when you messed up. If you don't think this is true, ask a trusted friend or family member who knows you well. You might be pleasantly surprised at how they perceive you and the gifts you bring to the world.

How Do You Prepare for a Good Death?

Beyond appreciating the goodness in the life you have lived, preparing for a good death doesn't have to be complicated. And it's not too late to start. The best way to die with ease and grace is to live your life fully. I leave you with some suggestions for how to do that.

- Live each day fully and exuberantly. Do your best to notice moments to treasure in each day, and take time every morning or night to count your blessings. Literally. Naming them or writing them down helps you be aware of them.

- Be present and available in your relationships, and celebrate the joys of intimacy and collaboration with others.

- Be creative and seek out awe-inspiring experiences, especially those that involve the sensory worlds of art, music, dance and literature. Even as a spectator, you may discover that these activities open hearts by engaging the special nature of the human spirit.

- Spend time in nature and notice the relaxation and well-being that it brings you. See if you can focus on a specific aspect of nature, like clouds, waves, trees, birds, or rock formations.

• Seek connection with the spiritual through direct practice as well through sacred/philosophical readings that educate and inspire you. Figure out what you believe in! Find a spiritual community with others who share your beliefs. Practicing your faith with others, especially through prayer, enhances and expands individual experience.

Enjoy Your Life

Above all, relax! Try not to worry about the end of life. As Abraham Lincoln famously said, "In the end, it's not the years in your life that count. It's the life in your years." Explore what that can mean for you, and really find out what it means to *be* you. Keep a positive attitude. And remember this: wherever you go, you are never truly alone.

Bibliography

Books

Bastian, Edward and Staley, Tina. *Living Fully Dying Well* (2009) Boulder, CO: Sounds True, Inc.

Byock, Ira. *Four Things that Matter Most* (2004) New York, NY: Simon and Schuster

Callahan, Maggie and Kelly, Patricia. *Final Gifts* (1992) New York, NY: Simon and Schuster

Greyson, Bruce. *After* (2021) New York, NY: St. Martin's Essentials

Kalanithi, Paul. *When Breath Becomes Air* (2016) New York, NY: Random House Inc.

Levine, Stephen. *A Year to Live* (1997) New York, NY: Random House, Inc.

Levine, Stephen. *Who Dies?* (1982) New York, NY: Doubleday Dell Publishing Group, Inc.

Lipsenthal, Lee. *Enjoy Every Sandwich* (2011) New York, NY: MJF Books/Fine Communications

McEntyre, Marilyn Chandler. *A Faithful Farewell: Living your Last Chapter with Love* (2015) Grand Rapids, MI: Wm. B. Eerdmans Publishing Co.

McNees, Pat. *Dying – A Book of Comfort* (1996) New York, NY: Doubleday Direct, Inc.

Plato, *Five Dialogues,Phaedo*

Schlitz, Marilyn. *Death Makes Life Possible* (2015) Louisville, CO: Sounds True, Inc.

Singh, Kathleen Dowling. *The Grace in Aging* (2014) Somerville, MA: Wisdom Publications

Speerstra, Karen and Anderson, Herbert. *The Divine Art of Dying* (2014) Studio City, CA: Michael Wiese Productions

Wyatt, Karen M. *What Really Matters* (2011) Silverthorne, CO: Sunroom Studios

Publications

Advanced health care directive (state-specific):
http://www.caringinfo.org

POLST form: http://polst.org/

5 Wishes form: https://www.agingwithdignity.org/

About the Author

First-time author Sue Hagan lived through profound personal experiences including a Near Death Experience (NDE), completed a Certificate in Thanatology and participated in various mindfulness, caregiving and conscious dying programs addressing end-of-life issues. Drawing on personal spiritual insights, she shares her message of comfort and support to those who are seriously ill and wondering what comes next.

Suehagan.com